Your Burro Is No Jackass!

Other Avon Camelot Books by
Jim Aylward

You're Dumber in the Summer

JIM AYLWARD is a well-known radio personality in New York City, and is also a newspaper columnist for United Feature Syndicate. His popular feature "Things No One Ever Tells You" started on radio, was extended to newspapers across the country, and now appears as a book for young readers.

Your Burro Is No Jackass!

And Over 100 Other Things No One Ever Told You

Jim Aylward

Illustrated by Laura Hartman

AN AVON  CAMELOT BOOK

6th grade reading level has been determined by using the Fry Readability Scale.

AVON BOOKS
A division of
The Hearst Corporation
959 Eighth Avenue
New York, New York 10019

The Holt, Rinehart and Winston edition contains the following Library of Congress Cataloging in Publication Data:

Aylward, Jim
Your burro is no jackass!
Summary: A collection of unusual facts, figures,
and feats, such as the number of calories used
while playing the piano, a goat's favorite dinner,
and the size of the heaviest hog.
1. Curiosities and wonders—Juvenile literature.
[1. Curiosities and wonders] I. Hartman, Laura.
II. Title.   AG243.A88   031′.02   81-4603
AACR2

First Camelot Printing, June, 1983

Printed in the U.S.A.

DON 10 9 8 7 6 5 4 3 2 1

To Terrye Wax,
a dear friend who once said,
"You're no bunny
'till some bunny loves you!"

Contents

Pineapples, Sharks, Armadillos and Lassie

◆

Alligators love marshmallows.

* * *

Snow can be bright red, pink, yellow, green or blue. Most of those colors are seen at higher altitudes, where various organisms live in the snow.

* * *

Raspberries and strawberries aren't really berries. They belong to the rose family.

A pineapple isn't an apple. It's a berry. A pineberry.

* * *

If your name is Jim Smith you can join the Society of Jim Smiths. The organization has some 1,000 members worldwide, all named Jim Smith. Four of them are women. By the way, the founder of the Society of Jim Smiths is Jim Smith.

* * *

The very first Lassie was named Pal. Pal, come home?

An armadillo can bury himself in just two minutes in earth so hard your Uncle Phil would need a pick ax to chop through it.

* * *

More than 220 Rhode Islands could fit into just one Texas.

The shark is nature's vacuum cleaner. Sharks eat bottles, tin cans, magazines, old clothes, anchors, boat propellers, lead sinkers and logs. And, if the moon is full, Americans, Norwegians, Lithuanians . . .

Gelatin is good for houseplants. Watering plants once a month with unflavored gelatin and four cups of water makes them grow better and produces lush foliage. Cherry, orange, lemon and fern.

A teaspoon of sugar may make the medicine go down, but one teaspoon may not be the same size as another. Teaspoons in silverware sets vary in size from maker to maker. If it's important to get exactly one teaspoon of medicine, a doctor will recommend buying one at a pharmacy. Mary Poppins, please note.

The average human (that could be you!) walks 19,000 steps every day. When you get up tomorrow keep count.

The civil defense director of Bald Eagle, Pennsylvania, is Donald Duck. Not the one with feathers and the nephews. This one is a man whose NAME is Donald Duck.

* * *

Playing the piano can use more calories than gymnastic exercises.

When a sloth eats, it takes him almost two weeks to digest his meal. Sloths are slow.

Rollerskates, Indians, Eagles and Cougars

If Thomas Jefferson hadn't been a statesman, he would have been remembered as the man who invented the swivel chair. Thank Tom for that.

The word "tuxedo" comes from an Algonquin Indian word that used to mean "he has a round foot." It still means that today, but it doesn't come up much in conversation.

* * *

Your Baby Ruth candy bar wasn't named for Babe Ruth, the famous baseball star. It was named for President Grover Cleveland's daughter.

* * *

The United States has its own version of Italy's Leaning Tower of Pisa. Our own Washington Monument is settling into the ground at the rate of about a half foot per century. That means it will disappear entirely by the year 113073. You'll probably miss that.

There are 22 kinds of plants that will grow only in Death Valley. The unusual plants are of great interest to scientists. They include varieties of cactus and mesquite as well as desert shrubs and grasses.

* * *

If your cat lives a good, long life, it'll add up to more than $1,500. in cat food. That's a lot of num-nums.

Teenagers spend more time listening to the radio than watching TV. The average teen spends nearly three hours a day now listening to the radio.

* * *

Sixty-five percent of rollerskating injuries are fractures and dislocations. Protective clothing, wrist guards, knee and elbow pads, and even mouth guards can help keep you from skating to the emergency room.

At the rate of one drop each second, a dripping faucet can waste 900 gallons of water in one year.

* * *

If your eyes were as large as an eagle's in proportion to your body weight, they would weigh several pounds each. Most eagles can see eight times better than you can. In fact, a soaring eagle can spot a rabbit two miles away. That's what adults mean when they say someone is "eagle-eyed."

* * *

They say you "see red" when you lose your temper. If YOU see red you'd better get into "the pink" fast. Scientists say the color pink can actually make you quiet and peaceful. You can change a cougar into a pussycat if you get him into "the pink."

* * *

If you think Laverne and Shirley are "crazy" here, in Thailand, where women never talk back or make jokes, the *Laverne and Shirley* program is shown with a notice telling viewers that the two are actually inmates from a mental hospital.

Outer Space, Ice Cream, Streetcars and Gophers

Corn-flavored ice cream is a favorite in South America.

* * *

The movie-makers have it all wrong when they show us creatures from outer space. David Hines, a NASA researcher, says intelligent aliens aren't blobs or giant mosquitos or clawed tigers. He says they probably look like six-legged horses!

If standing up in class and reading an essay is as difficult for you as making a trip to the dentist, you're not alone. Most adults don't like talking before a group either. Public speaking is America's biggest fear today.

At the turn of the century, New Yorkers could travel by streetcar all the way to Boston for less than $4. The longest nonstop streetcar route in those days ran from Freeport, Illinois, to Utica, New York—a distance of more than 1,000 miles.

When children are asked to draw their parents as animals they almost always draw Dad as a lion and Mom as a bird.

Early American colonists made gray paint for their houses by boiling blueberries in milk.

* * *

Between the ages of 20 and 70, the average person spends at least five years just standing in lines.

A jet plane has a point right behind the engine's exhaust where no sound at all is registered.

* * *

A pound of raw shelled peanuts contains as much protein as two pounds of sirloin steak or four quarts of milk.

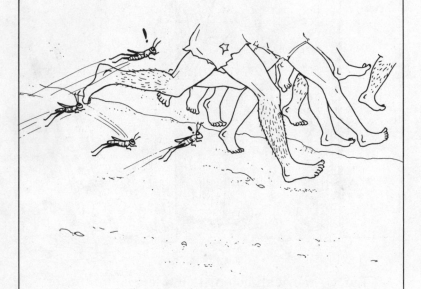

When swarms of grasshoppers have devoured all plant life, they'll eat paint off your house, chew your clothing and Mom's curtains and, if they get a chance, your ankles and elbows.

The polar bear doesn't need overshoes in the winter. Polar bears have fur on the soles of their feet.

OLD BEAR-FOOT IN A PARKA

Monaco has a national orchestra larger than its army. The orchestra has 85 members, and the army has only 82. Make music, not war.

* * *

If you have a cavy running around the house, you have a guinea pig. A cavy is an animal without a tail and does most of its eating at night. During the *Late Show*.

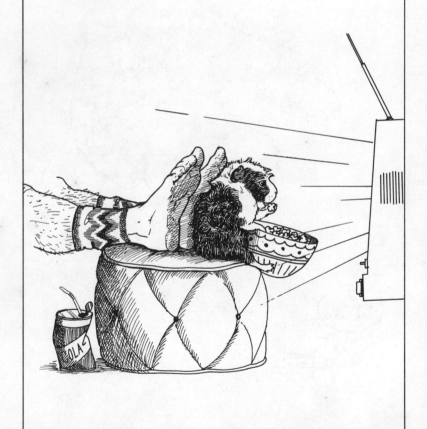

North Dakota is known as the Flickertail State.
A flickertail is a gopher, and in North Dakota a
gopher just loves to flick 'er tail.

Hiccups, Dandelions, Goats and Big Bird

Fish swim backwards. If they want to.

* * *

A girl's memory is 8 percent better than a boy's memory . . . but I forget why.

* * *

Rolling naked in the snow is supposed to be a good cure for hiccups. It's not too good for the flu, but then, what is?

Cockroaches were introduced into America from Europe and were once known as Croton bugs. They first became common around water pipes in New York City apartments around 1842, when the aqueduct carrying water from the Croton River was completed. New York has been bugged with them ever since.

The word "dandelion" comes from the French *dent de lion*, or "lion's tooth." It was named for the jagged leaves that look something like the teeth of lions. If you think I'm lyin', dandy!

* * *

Paper, just like the paper this page is made of, comes from trees. It takes thousands of trees to print the Sunday edition of the *New York Times*.

* * *

The hottest day ever in the United States must have been July 10, 1913. On that date the temperature recorded at Death Valley, California, was 138 degrees.

When you get to be 30 years old not only will you be "over the hill," but you will have spent 12 years of your life fast asleep.

* * *

Sesame Street characters outsell Disney characters in the big money toy industry. Big Bird and Kermit are driving Mickey and Donald goofy.

* * *

Your goat's favorite dinner is the tender, new shoots produced by shrubs and herbs. Goats like young, green leaves so much they will even eat poison ivy.

HE'S IN THE
POISON IVY
LEAGUE

If your name is John Smith, your Japanese name would probably be Minoru Suzuki. Just as our telephone book is filled with people named John Smith, Tokyo's telephone directory lists hundreds of Minoru Suzukis. By the way, if you think your phone book is heavy, the Tokyo directory has 9,248 pages, comes in nine volumes and weighs 26 pounds.

Robots, Teddy Bears, Crackers and Gold

Crows live longer than any other bird. Your old crow just goes on and on.

* * *

No person who was an only child has ever been elected President of the United States. Franklin D. Roosevelt was indeed the only child of James and Sara Roosevelt, but James had been married to Rebecca Roosevelt before Sara, and they had a boy of their own, making F.D.R. a half brother.

If you fly your kite higher than 50 feet you must file a flight plan with the Federal Aviation Administration. If you fly a kite at sunrise or sunset you must have lights on it.

* * *

The average bumblebee has a stinger three thousand, one hundred twenty-five ten thousandths of an inch in length. The other four inches are just your imagination.

Your teachers are probably still telling you today that the four basic food groups are milk, meat, fruits and vegetables, and cereal grains. But in a new student poll, four different groups turned up. When asked to name the four basic food groups one student said, "McDonald's, Wendy's, Burger Chef and Pizza Hut!"

* * *

Hot water is heavier than cold water.

* * *

Graham crackers were developed by Sylvester Graham, a vegetarian who lectured on dietary reform across the United States in the first half of the 19th century. You can thank Sylvester for your grahams.

* * *

Eighty feet below the street, in the vaults of the Federal Reserve Bank of New York, lie 13,000 tons of gold, worth 101 billion dollars. That's more than twice the amount stored at Fort Knox.

Robot pets are in your future. The United States Robotics Society says they will be furry and will sit, bark and beg on command. When they get tired, they'll go back to a wall socket and recharge themselves. And they'll just love Robot Chow.

Your Daddy may have chosen your Mother as his wife because she reminded him of his teddy bear. Dr. Simon Grolnick says we often are attracted to people who remind us of childhood pets, security blankets or teddy bears.

* * *

The artificial sweetener saccharin is just over 100 years old. Happy birthday, sweetie!

When children in ancient Egypt suffered an illness, their doting parents immediately fed them skinned mice.

* * *

Medical research shows that when you sneeze, between 2,000 and 5,000 atomized droplets are expelled at a speed of more than 100 feet per second, and travel as far as 6 feet. That's a sneeze!

Burros are very smart. They can open gates that are latched. They can turn on water faucets in parks when they're thirsty. They can dig for water, too, and that's something a horse won't do. They can also eat almost anything and can live over 50 years. Your burro is no jackass!

Falcons, Hogs,
Zebras and Shrews

A falcon can see a ladybug on the sidewalk from atop an 18-story building. Falcons must have eyes like hawks.

* * *

The average American eats 90 pounds of sugar each year. Most of it is hidden in canned and frozen foods and soft drinks. If you check the ingredients on your favorite soup label, chances are you'll find "sugar."

If you have a lot of S.I., you don't need a high I.Q. S.I. is "social intelligence," or common sense—a quality that allows you to get along better in the world. Sometimes highly intelligent people don't do as well in day-to-day relationships as less-educated folks with a lot of S.I.

* * *

The heaviest hog on record was not a member of your family. It was a pig in North Carolina that weighed 1,904 pounds. That's a big pig. It weighed about the same as a Volkswagen Beetle.

In early prayer books and church almanacs the saints' days and religious festivals were printed in red ink. That's why we call them "red letter days."

* * *

Before it was that dark brown color, Coca Cola was a heavenly green.

* * *

They will never admit it, but most zebras spend all day long just sleeping on their feet.

Almost any short-tailed shrew can eat his weight in bugs every 24 hours.

A mosquito's favorite aroma is after-shave. They go after after-shave.

* * *

When George III of England wrote in his diary on July 4, 1776 he entered these now almost forgotten words: "Nothing of importance happened today."

* * *

Christmas dinner in a good restaurant in the year 1878 ran as high as $1.50. Outrageous!

* * *

The bullwhip makes a cracking noise because the tip moves faster than the speed of sound. The crack is actually a small sonic boom.

Snails, Whales, Cornmeal and Figs

A bamboo shoot can grow more than 3 feet in 24 hours.

* * *

The first mansion to house a presidential family was located at the corner of Franklin and Cherry streets in New York City. George and Martha Washington lived there.

A bee can fly at a speed of 60 miles per hour. That's honey power.

* * *

Cornmeal is usually yellow or white, but it may also be red, black or blue.

* * *

A garden snail has more than 14,000 teeth. They're arranged in 135 rows of 105 each. I bet a good orthodontist could work on one snail for the rest of his life.

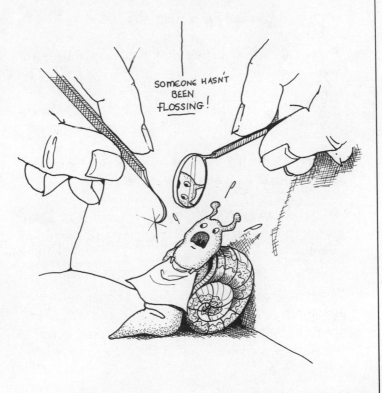

47

March, February, April? Until the year 1752, March was the FIRST month on the calendar.

* * *

In the winter we sprinkle four times as much salt on our streets as we do on our food.

* * *

A typical dinner for a whale is 5,000 fish.

* * *

Frown 200,000 times and you've produced a wrinkle.

* * *

A bat's knees bend backwards. Belfry experts say that's true.

* * *

While Holland is famous for tulips, the number-one flower there is the rose.

* * *

There are over 700 different types of figs. They range in color from whitish yellow to purple to black.

There are as many chickens in the United States today as there are people in this old world.

The United States Consumer Product Safety Commission is very concerned with toy safety. It ordered 80,000 buttons with the slogan "Think Toy Safety." The buttons, however, were found to be too dangerous to distribute. The pins had sharp points, the clips could be easily broken, and the paint contained a high quantity of lead.

* * *

If you tend to get carsick, don't ride in the back seat. Dr. Edward Schor says carsick kids have fewer problems if they're moved to the front seat or put in an elevated seat in the back. The doctor says you feel better in a car when you can see the horizon.

* * *

In the summertime the beautiful fallow deer sports a tan coat spotted with white. See that same deer again a few months later and you might not recognize him. He turns gray in the winter.

Lobsters, Cowhands, Bananas and Kangaroos

If you give a lobster a lot of love and attention it will live to be 50 years old.

* * *

One in every 29 people has an extra rib. You'll have to find out who they are yourself because I don't have all their names.

Your average canary is the proud owner of 2,200 feathers.

The song with the longest title in pop music history was recorded in 1961. It was called "Green With Envy, Purple With Passion, White With Anger, Scarlet With Fever, What Were You Doing in Her Arms Last Night Blues."

* * *

If your hair is blonde most people think of you as attractive, successful, and happy, but that old "dumb blonde" image still persists today. Attractive, successful, happy . . . and dumb.

* * *

The sea urchin has 5 sharp teeth, strong enough to dig holes in rocks or even to walk on.

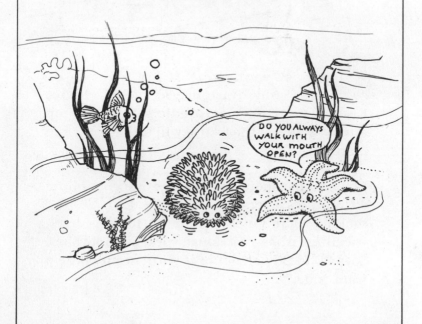

FIRST CITY BANK

While most youngsters today want to be cowhands and firefighters, the Michigan Employment Service predicts that the top growth fields of the future will be banking and plumbing.

* * *

Your mother spends an average of six hours and 49 minutes every day washing your clothes, making your lunch, shopping for groceries, washing dishes, etc. Housework! Good old Mom does 80 to 90 percent of it without much help from you.

Russian athletes don't look at films of their past accomplishments. They look at films of the "future," simulated motion pictures that show them accomplishing feats no one ever dreamed could happen. These mental movie experiments, the Russians say, are achieving encouraging results. What our minds can see, our bodies can achieve.

* * *

Next time you peel a banana, do it gently. Every banana in the world uses its skin to breathe. They inhale oxygen, exhale carbon dioxide and generate their own heat. What's yellow and holds its breath?

The congo snake does more than wriggle. It whistles as well. It doesn't tap dance, though. It just whistles.

Your dog's teeth should be brushed at least three times a week with a soft brush and tooth powder.

Your kingfisher is a yoke-toed bird. Two toes point forward, and two toes point back. Often the kingfisher will just stand looking at his toes and wondering which way to go.

* * *

A kangaroo can cruise at 12 to 15 miles per hour and can accelerate to more than twice that speed.

Pawpaws, Panthers, Llamas and Wahoo

A marsh rabbit can swim as easily as a duck. Any rabbit can swim if it wants to, but a marsh rabbit loves to backstroke among lily pads.

* * *

Wagga Wagga is not something Lassie's tail does. Wagga Wagga is a city in Australia.

* * *

A mole's ear is not like a human's ear. A mole's ear is a hole in the head. Since a mole's body was designed for digging, human-type ears would just get in the way.

The first successful parachute jump was made in the year 1797. That's probably why you don't remember it.

* * *

If you mix a little mayonnaise and celery with some wahoo you can have a nutritious sandwich filling for lunch. The wahoo is a tropical fish and a cousin of the tuna. Wahoo on whole wheat is neat.

* * *

A panther is not really a panther. It's actually a leopard or a puma. The cat experts say there isn't any animal properly known as a panther. Next time you come face to face with a panther, tell him he doesn't exist.

The earliest known vending machine was a coin-operated device that dispensed holy water in Greece in the third century B.C.

Otters hum. They don't sing or whistle, but they hum. Some otters even hum in their sleep. Hmmmm-z-z-z-z-z.

The very first washing machine was cranked out (literally) in 1859. Hamilton E. Smith of Pennsylvania patented his miraculous Mom-saving invention, which was a washtub and a series of paddles. A hand crank moved the paddles, and the paddles moved the water and the clothes. Mom moved the hand crank. And she's been cranky about washing machines ever since.

Llamas have bad tempers. They hiss and bite. A llama may llook lloving, but it's not.

A pawpaw is not somebody's daddy. A pawpaw is a small fruit tree producing banana-like fruit. In the Midwest a pawpaw is called a custard apple.

* * *

Rocks near the Arctic Circle in Greenland are the oldest things ever found on Earth—3.8 billion years old. The only things older either landed here from space, like meteorites, or were brought back from the moon.

* * *.

Each eye of a chameleon moves separately. Without moving or turning its head, a chameleon can look in two directions at once. That's why it's so hard for a chameleon to get a driver's license in Connecticut.